1/12

First Facts

First Cookbooks

A Christmas
COOKBOOK

Simple Recipes for Kids

by Sarah L. Schuette

First Facts is published by Capstone Press,
151 Good Counsel Drive, P.O. Box 669, Mankato, Minnesota 56002.
www.capstonepub.com

 Books published by Capstone Press are manufactured with paper
containing at least 10 percent post-consumer waste.

Library of Congress Cataloging-in-Publication Data
Schuette, Sarah L., 1976–
  A Christmas cookbook : simple recipes for kids / by Sarah L. Schuette.
     p. cm. — (First facts. First cookbooks)
  Includes bibliographical references and index.
  Summary: "Provides instructions and step-by-step photos for making a variety of simple snacks with a
Christmas theme"— Provided by publisher.
  ISBN 978-1-4296-5999-4 (library binding)
  1. Christmas cooking—Juvenile literature. 2. Cookbooks—Juvenile literature. I. Title.
  TX739.2.C45S38 2012
  641.5'686—dc22
                                   2011001803

Editorial Credits
Christine Peterson editor; Heidi Thompson, designer; Sarah Schuette, photo stylist; Marcy Morin, studio
     scheduler; Laura Manthe, production specialist

Photo Credits
All images Capstone Studio/Karon Dubke except:
Shutterstock: cloki, cover (gold bulb); eedology, red holiday background; Gorilla, fir tree design; Kapu,
cover (blue bulb)

The author dedicates this book to her mother, Jane Schuette, for always making Christmas
a joyous holiday full of giving.

Printed in the United States of America in Stevens Point, Wisconsin.
082011
006349R

Table of Contents

Festive Foods!

Merry Christmas! Happy Holidays! No matter the greeting, the holiday season is full of celebrations. And celebrations mean food. Drive your **sleigh** into the kitchen and whip up some festive treats.

Even Santa and his elves plan ahead for Christmas Eve. Read your recipes carefully. Make your **ingredient** list, and check it twice. Ask an adult if you have questions.

Remember to wash your hands, and clean up when you're finished. A clean kitchen will get you on Santa's nice list.

Metric Conversion Chart	
United States	**Metric**
¼ teaspoon	1.2 mL
½ teaspoon	2.5 mL
1 teaspoon	5 mL
1 tablespoon	15 mL
¼ cup	60 mL
⅓ cup	80 mL
½ cup	120 mL
⅔ cup	160 mL
¾ cup	175 mL
1 cup	240 mL
1 ounce	30 gms

5

Tools

Think of your kitchen as Santa's workshop. It's filled with everything you will need for cooking. Use this guide to choose the perfect tools.

cutting board—a wooden or plastic board used when slicing or chopping foods

liquid measuring cup—a glass or plastic measuring cup with a spout for pouring

measuring cups—round cups with handles used for measuring dry ingredients

measuring spoons—spoons with small deep scoops used to measure both wet and dry ingredients

mixing bowl—a sturdy bowl used for mixing ingredients

Techniques

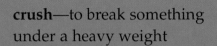

crush—to break something under a heavy weight

drizzle—to let a liquid fall in small amounts

fold—to mix ingredients gently by lifting a mixture up and over itself

measure—to take a specific amount of something

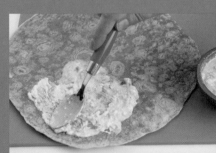

spread—to cover a surface with something

sprinkle—to scatter something in small drops or bits

stir—to mix something by moving a spoon around in it

toss—to mix gently with two spoons or forks

rolling pin—a kitchen tool shaped like a cylinder that is used to flatten dough or crush ingredients

rubber scraper—a kitchen tool with a rubber paddle on one end

North Pole Pie

When Mrs. Claus needs peppermint for a recipe, she picks candy canes! **Legend** says that candy canes hang from pine trees at the North Pole. Make this minty chocolate treat with your leftover candy canes.

Makes 1 pie

Ingredients:
- 1 large candy cane
- 1 8-ounce container of whipped chocolate yogurt
- ¼ cup whipped topping
- 1 4-inch mini graham cracker piecrust

Tools:
- zip-top bag
- rolling pin
- spoon
- mixing bowl
- measuring cups

TIP:
You can freeze this pie for a cooler treat. Just cover the pie with plastic wrap and put it into the freezer for two hours.

1 Place candy cane in zip-top bag. Crush candy cane into small pieces with a rolling pin.

2 Scoop yogurt into bowl.

3 Measure whipped topping and add to yogurt.

4 With a spoon, combine yogurt and whipped topping.

5 Spoon yogurt mixture into a piecrust.

6 Sprinkle candy cane pieces on top of the pie. Refrigerate pie for one hour before serving.

Blitzen's Bagels

Santa's speedy deliveries depend on his **reindeer**. Luckily Blitzen is as fast as lightning. And you can be too. You can make these colorful snacks in a flash!

Makes 2 bagel halves

Ingredients:
- 1 whole-wheat bagel, split
- 1 wedge soft Swiss cheese
- 2 lettuce leaves
- 2 tomato slices

Tools:
- toaster
- plate
- spoon
- knife

1 Have an adult help you toast the bagel. Then place the bagel halves on a plate.

2 With the spoon, spread cheese on each bagel piece.

3 Top bagels with lettuce leaves.

4 Have an adult slice a tomato. Add tomato slice to each bagel.

TIP:
Not a fan of tomatoes? Try slices of fresh mozzarella cheese and red pepper strips.

Hawaiian Snowball Salad

If you spend Christmas in Hawaii, you won't see snow. But you can imagine shredded coconut as falling snowflakes. Or picture marshmallows as snowballs. Now enjoy a **tropical** holiday with this fruity salad.

Makes 2 servings

Ingredients:
- 2 apples
- ½ teaspoon lemon juice
- 1 cup miniature marshmallows
- ½ cup shredded coconut
- 1 8-ounce container vanilla low-fat yogurt
- ¼ cup low-fat mayonnaise
- ¼ teaspoon sugar

Tools:
- knife
- 2 mixing bowls
- measuring spoons
- 2 spoons
- measuring cups
- rubber scraper

TIP:
Need more crunch? Stir in some walnuts and chopped celery.

1 Have an adult cut apples into small pieces. Place apple pieces into a mixing bowl.

2 Measure lemon juice, and pour over apples. Toss lightly to mix.

3 Measure marshmallows and coconut, and add to the apples. Mix ingredients together with a spoon.

4 In a second bowl, measure and combine yogurt, mayonnaise, and sugar.

5 Use a rubber scraper to fold yogurt mixture into fruit. Refrigerate before serving.

Santa's Salsa Rolls

Santa gets tired of cookies by the end of Christmas Eve night. He'll have a jolly laugh when he spots these spicy rolls waiting for him. Don't forget a glass of milk!

Makes 12-20 rolls

Ingredients:

- 3 tablespoons salsa
- ¼ teaspoon chili powder
- 1 8-ounce container whipped cream cheese
- 2 spinach tortillas
- ⅓ cup shredded cheese

Tools:

- small bowl
- measuring spoons
- spoon
- cutting board
- measuring cups
- knife

1 In a small bowl, measure salsa, chili powder, and cream cheese. Mix ingredients together with a spoon.

2 Place tortillas on a cutting board. With a spoon, spread half of the cream cheese mixture on each tortilla.

3 Measure shredded cheese, and sprinkle half on each tortilla.

4 Roll tortillas into a long tube. Have an adult cut the tortillas into 1-inch rolls.

TIP:
If you don't like salsa, you can use pizza sauce instead.

Stuffed Sleigh Sammies

On Christmas Eve morning, Santa stuffs the sleigh full of toys. He's too busy to stop for lunch. Stuffed **pitas** are a great meal for anyone on the go, even Santa!

Makes 1 sandwich

Ingredients:

- 1 pita bread half
- 3 chicken chunks
- 1 piece cheddar cheese
- 2 tomato slices
- shredded lettuce
- 1 tablespoon fat-free ranch dressing

Tools:

- plate
- knife
- spoon

1 Place pita half on a plate. Fill pita pocket with meat and cheese.

2 Have an adult slice a tomato. Add tomato slices to sandwich.

3 Sprinkle lettuce on top.

4 Using a spoon, drizzle your sandwich with dressing.

TIP:
Most any ingredient will work with pita bread. Try pitas with peanut butter and jelly or your favorite sandwich fixings.

Popcorn Garland

For **centuries**, people have decorated their Christmas trees with homemade **garlands**. Thread some popcorn, cranberries, and other treats together to make a fun snack. Or use it to decorate your tree.

Makes 1 garland

Ingredients:
- 1 bag microwave popcorn, plain
- 1 cup dried cranberries
- 1 cup dried cereal with hole in the middle
- 1 cup gumdrops

Tools:
- microwave
- 4 bowls
- measuring cups
- scissors
- thread
- needle

TIP:
Try other dried fruits, such as apples and apricots, on your garland.

18

1 Have an adult help you make popcorn in the microwave. Let popcorn cool in the bag before pouring it into a bowl.

2 Measure cranberries, cereal, and gumdrops, and put in separate bowls.

3 Cut a 4-foot (1.2 meter) piece of thread. Thread string through the needle. Tie the ends together.

4 With an adult's help, put the needle through the fluffy part of the popcorn. Slide the popcorn piece toward the knot. Repeat with a second piece of popcorn.

5 Thread cranberries, cereal, and gumdrops onto the garland. Push ingredients close together.

Mrs. Claus Cookies

All year long, Mrs. Claus bakes treats for Santa and the elves. When she needs a break from baking, she pulls out this recipe. No oven required!

Makes about 24 cookies

Ingredients:
- ½ cup peanut butter
- ½ cup honey
- ¼ cup frozen orange juice concentrate
- 1 ½ cups nonfat dry milk
- 1 teaspoon vanilla
- 2 cups oatmeal
- ½ cup mini chocolate chips

Tools:
- measuring cups
- mixing bowl
- measuring spoons
- spoon
- cutting board
- small drinking glass

1 Measure peanut butter and honey. Add ingredients to a mixing bowl.

2 Measure orange juice concentrate, powdered milk, and vanilla. Add ingredients to mixing bowl and stir.

3 Measure oatmeal and chocolate chips. Add to peanut butter mixture and stir.

4 With a spoon, stir ingredients to combine.

5 With clean hands, shape dough into 2-inch (5 centimeters) balls. Place dough balls on a cutting board.

6 Flatten balls with the bottom of a glass. Let cookies rest for one hour before serving.

Glossary

century (SEN-chuh-ree)—a period of 100 years

garland (GAR-luhnd)—a rope made from leaves, flowers, or other items

ingredient (in-GREE-dee-uhnt)—an item used to make something else

legend (LEJ-uhnd)—a story handed down from earlier times; legends are often based on fact, but they are not entirely true

pita (PEE-tuh)—a thin, flat bread that can be separated into two layers to form a pocket for meat, vegetables, and other fillings

reindeer (RAYN-dihr)—a type of deer that lives in the world's far northern regions

sleigh (SLAY)—a sled with runners designed to be pulled across the snow

tropical (TROP-uh-kuhl)—having to do with the hot and wet areas near the equator

Read More

Fauchald, Nick. *Indoor S'mores and Other Tasty Treats for Special Occasions.* Kids Dish. Minneapolis: Picture Window Books, 2008.

Lynette, Rachel. *Let's Throw A Christmas Party!* Holiday Parties. New York: PowerKids Press, 2011.

Internet Sites

FactHound offers a safe, fun way to find Internet sites related to this book. All of the sites on FactHound have been researched by our staff.

Here's all you do:

Visit *www.facthound.com*

Type in this code: 9781429659994

Super-cool stuff! Check out projects, games and lots more at **www.capstonekids.com**

Index